ACTIVITY BOOK 1

I0801098

WELCOME TO OUR WORLD

SECOND EDITION

SERIES EDITORS
Joan Kang Shin & JoAnn (Jodi) Crandall

NATIONAL GEOGRAPHIC
LEARNING

Australia • Brazil • Canada • Mexico • Singapore • United Kingdom • United States

HELLO!

Listen and circle. Say. **TR: AB.0.1**

Draw and say.

1 EYES, NOSE, MOUTH

VOCABULARY Look and say. Find and circle.

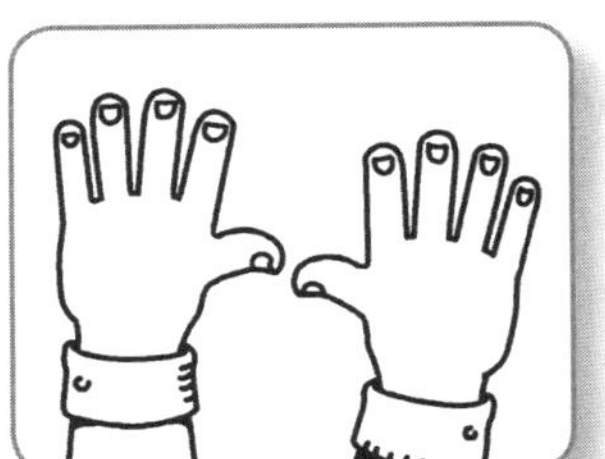

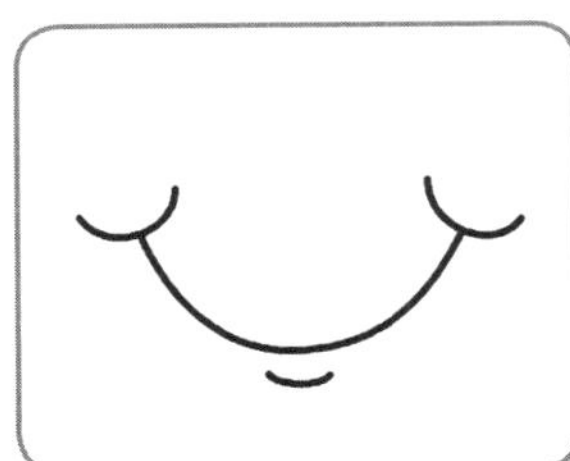

SONG Listen and draw. **TR: AB.1.1**

THE SOUNDS OF ENGLISH Listen and say. Circle. **TR: AB.1.2**

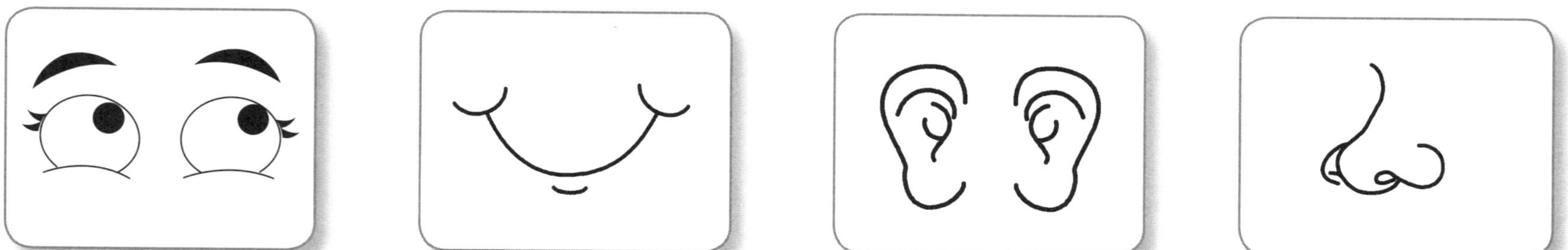

CONCEPTS Count and draw a line.

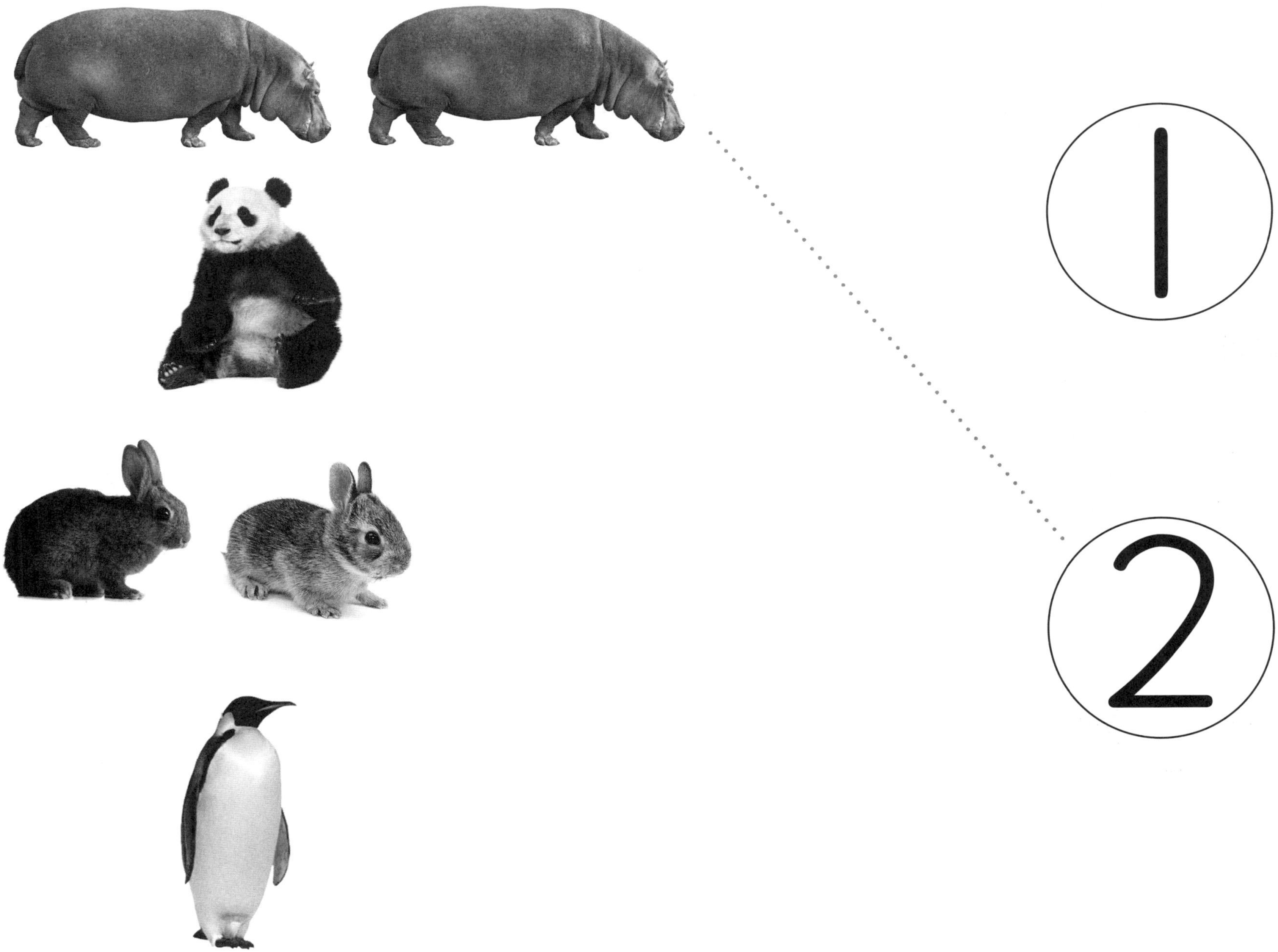

LANGUAGE IN USE Listen. Trace and say. Color. **TR: AB.1.3**

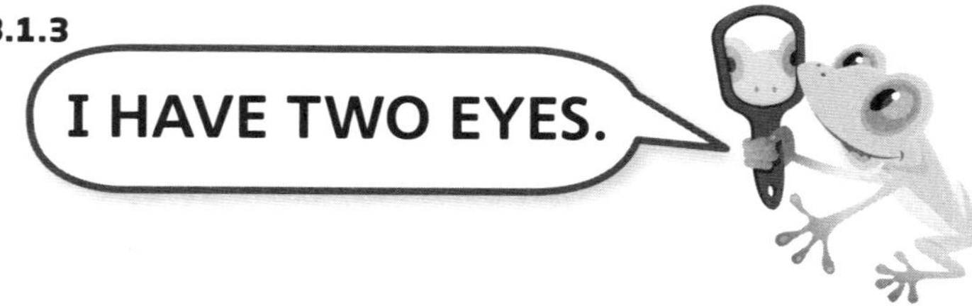

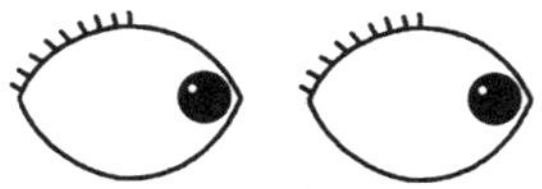

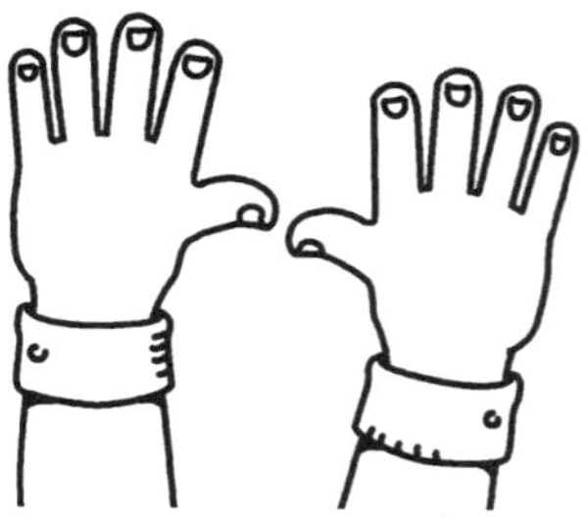

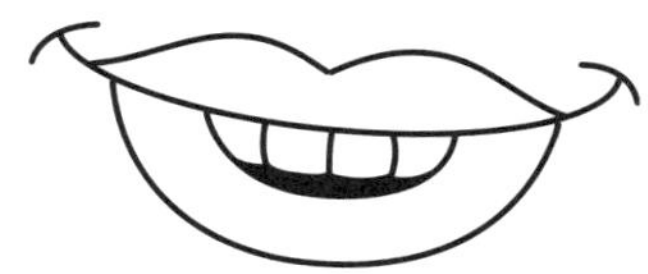

2 MY HOME

VOCABULARY Draw a line and say.

SONG Listen and circle. Color. TR: AB.2.1

THE SOUNDS OF ENGLISH Listen and say. Circle. TR: AB.2.2

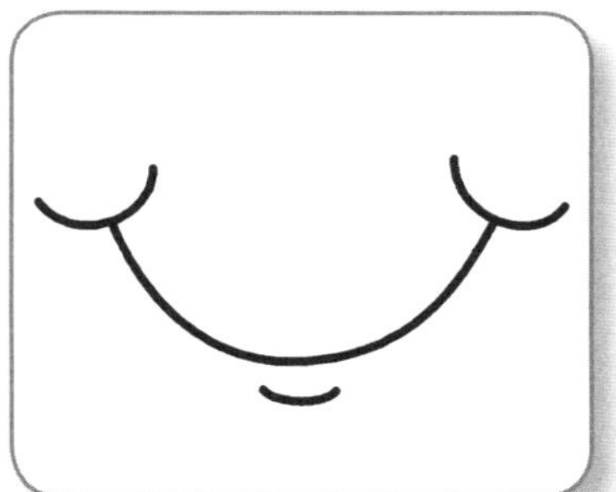

CONCEPTS Look and circle. Use red for open. Use blue for close.

LANGUAGE IN USE Listen. Trace and say. **TR: AB.2.3**

3 SNACK TIME

VOCABULARY

Point and say. Color.

SONG Find the bananas. Draw a line. **TR: AB.3.1**

THE SOUNDS OF ENGLISH Listen and say. Circle. **TR: AB.3.2**

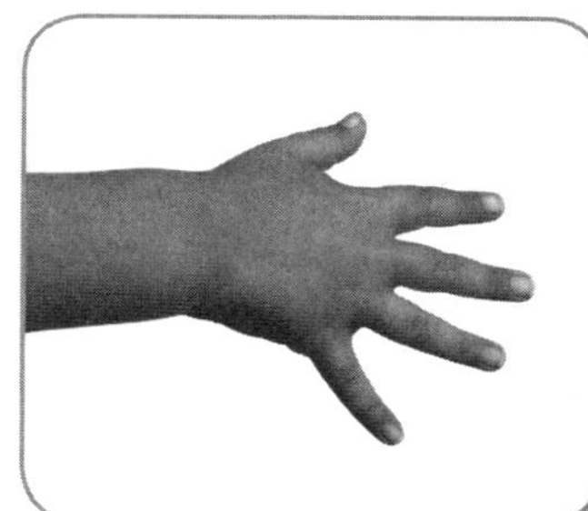

CONCEPTS Say. Draw and count.

5

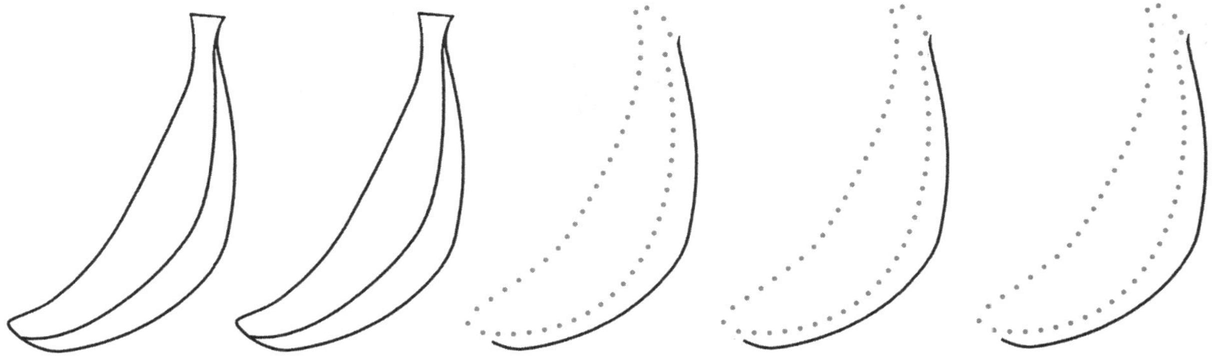

4

3

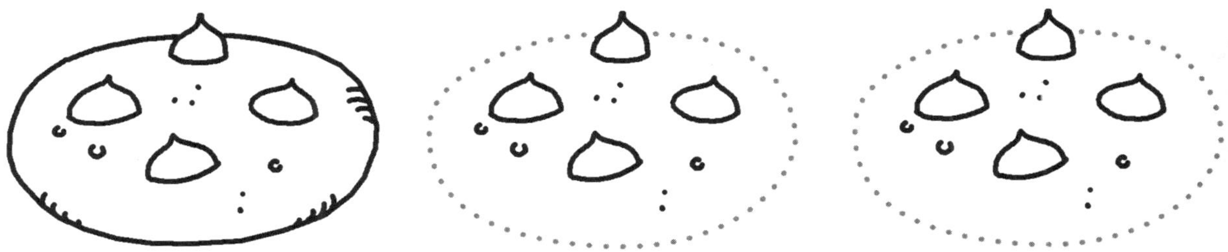

LANGUAGE IN USE Listen. Draw a line and say. **TR: AB.3.3**

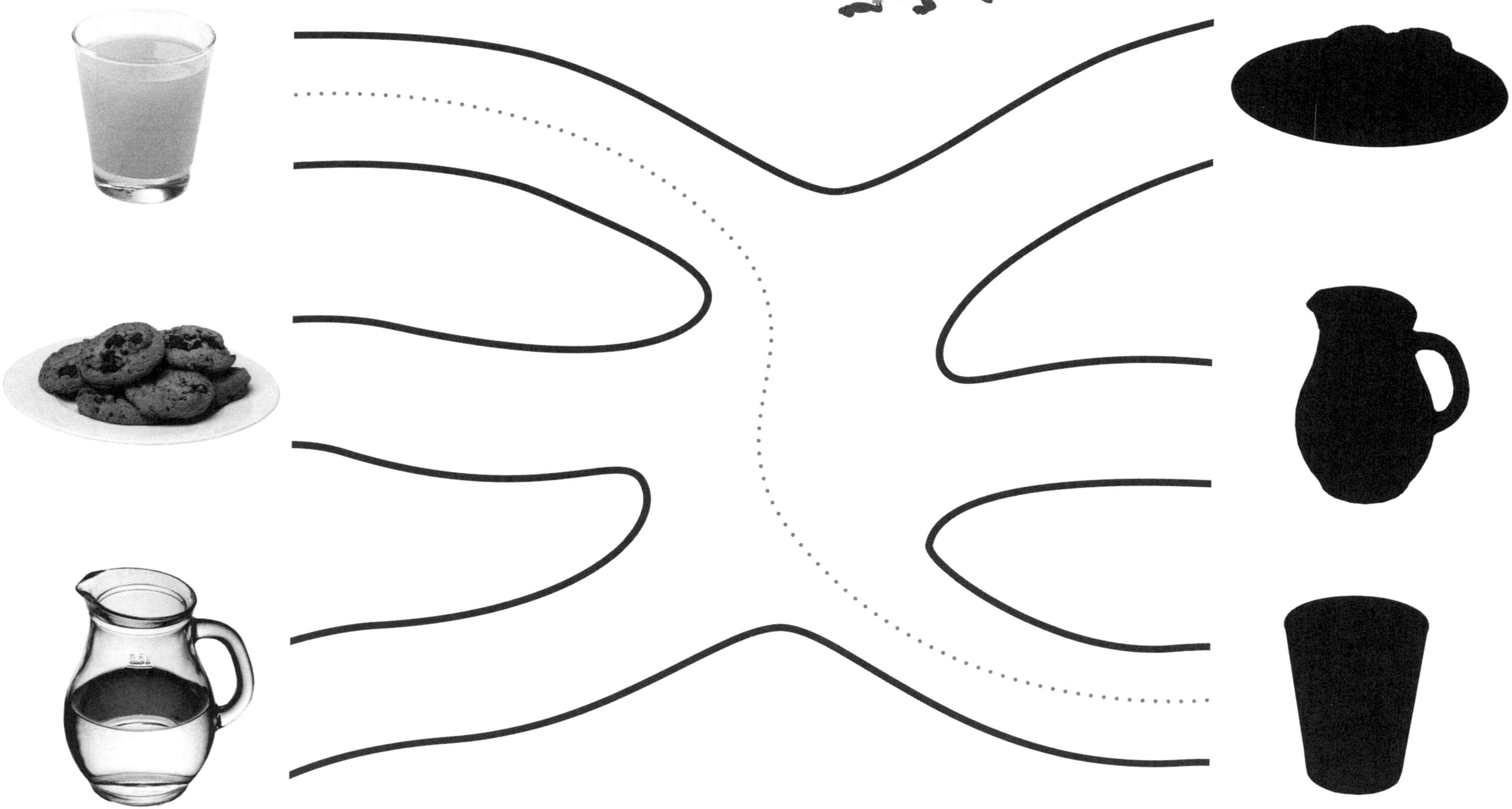

4 MY DRESS IS YELLOW

VOCABULARY Say and draw a line.

SONG Listen and color. **TR: AB.4.1**

THE SOUNDS OF ENGLISH Listen and say. Circle. **TR: AB.4.2**

CONCEPTS Color red, yellow, or blue. Say.

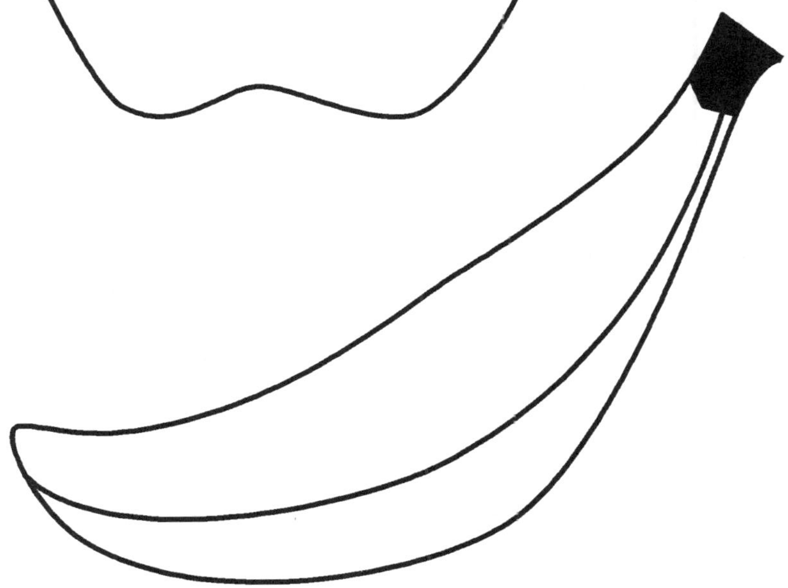

LANGUAGE IN USE Listen. Trace and color. Say. **TR: AB.4.3**

REVIEW

Find and color. Count and circle.

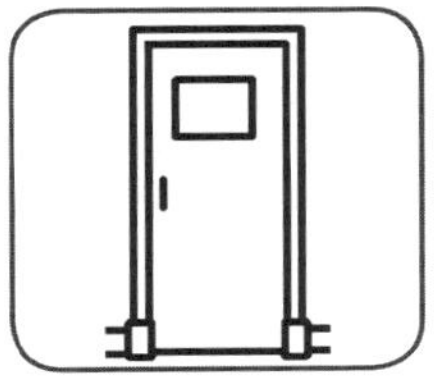

1 2 3 4 5

1 2 3 4 5

1 2 3 4 5

1 2 3 4 5

1 2 3 4 5

Trace. Color the clothes blue, red, and yellow. Say.

5 FAMILY

VOCABULARY Draw a line and say.

SONG Listen and draw. **TR: AB.5.1**

THE SOUNDS OF ENGLISH Listen and say. Circle. **TR: AB.5.2**

CONCEPTS Say and draw a line.

LANGUAGE IN USE Listen. Trace and say. **TR: AB.5.3**

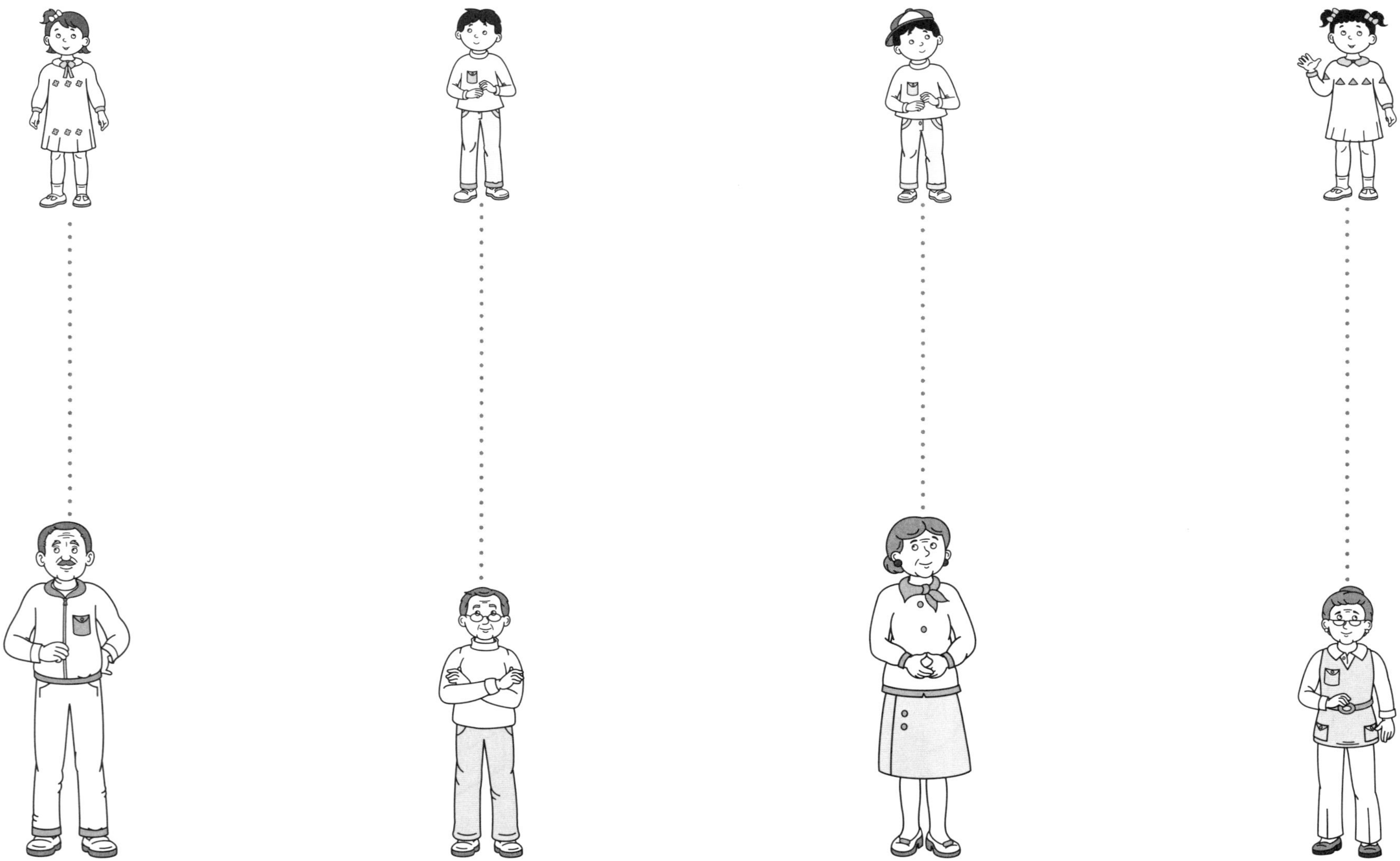

6 I LIKE TRAINS

VOCABULARY Listen and say. Circle. **TR: AB.6.1**

SONG Listen and color. **TR: AB.6.2**

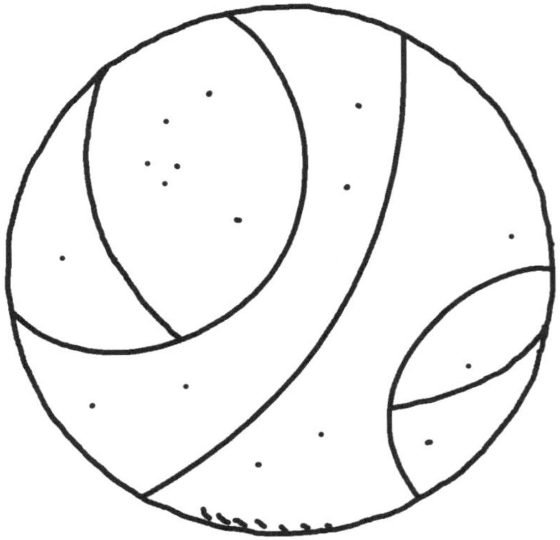

THE SOUNDS OF ENGLISH Listen and say. Circle. **TR: AB.6.3**

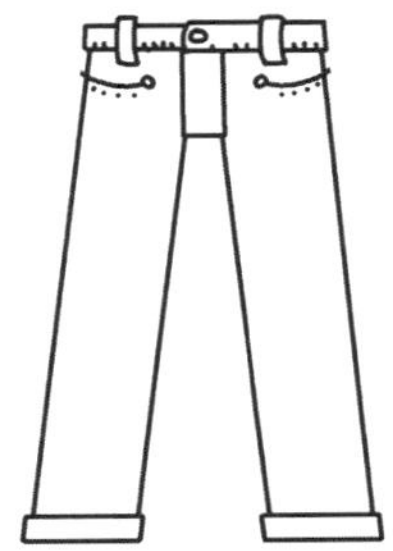

CONCEPTS Trace and draw a line. Say.

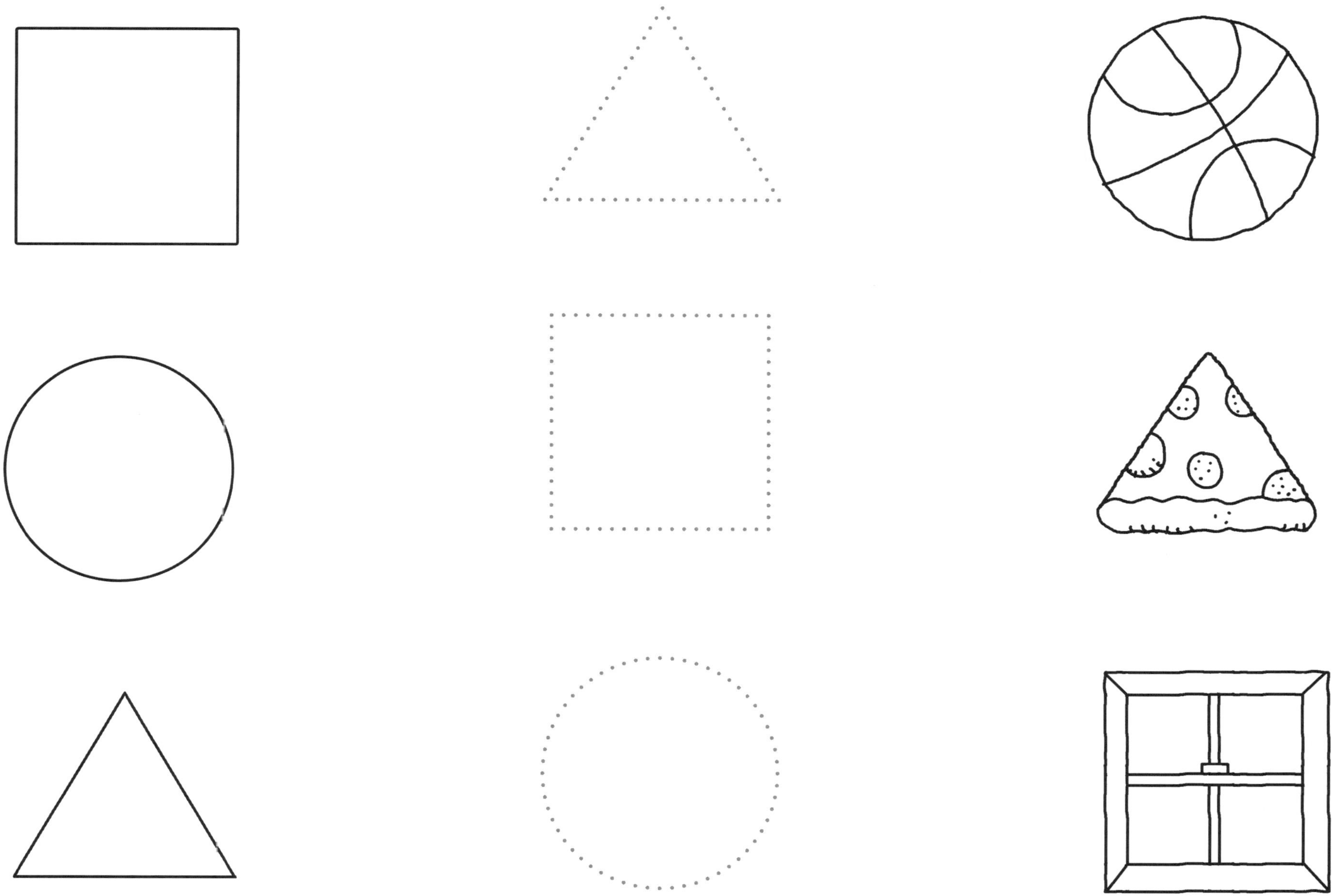

LANGUAGE IN USE Listen. Trace and say. **TR: AB.6.4**

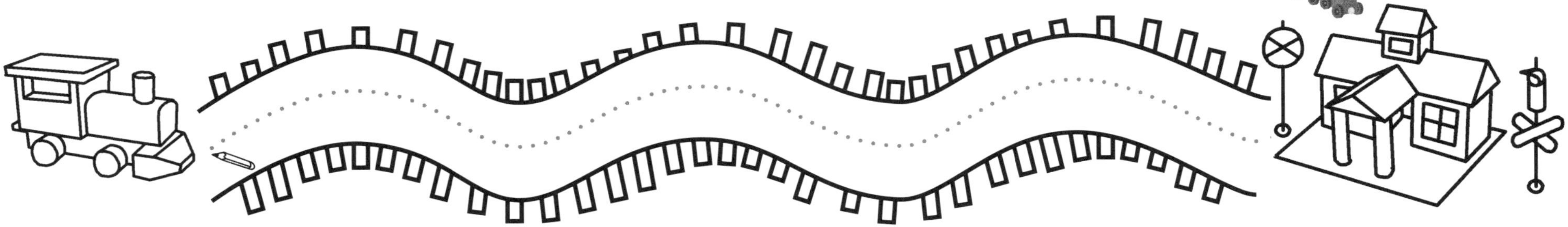

7 MY DOG IS SMALL

VOCABULARY Draw a line. Point and say.

SONG Listen and circle. **TR: AB.7.1**

THE SOUNDS OF ENGLISH Listen and say. Circle. **TR: AB.7.2**

CONCEPTS Look and say. Circle.

LANGUAGE IN USE Listen. Count and draw. Say and color. **TR: AB.7.3**

8 LOOK AT THE BUG!

VOCABULARY Draw a line and say.

SONG Listen. Choose and circle. Color. **TR: AB.8.1**

THE SOUNDS OF ENGLISH Listen and say. Circle. **TR: AB.8.2**

CONCEPTS Color the picture green, orange, pink, and purple. Say.

LANGUAGE IN USE Listen. Trace and say. **TR: AB.8.3**

REVIEW

Listen and color. **TR: AB.8.6**

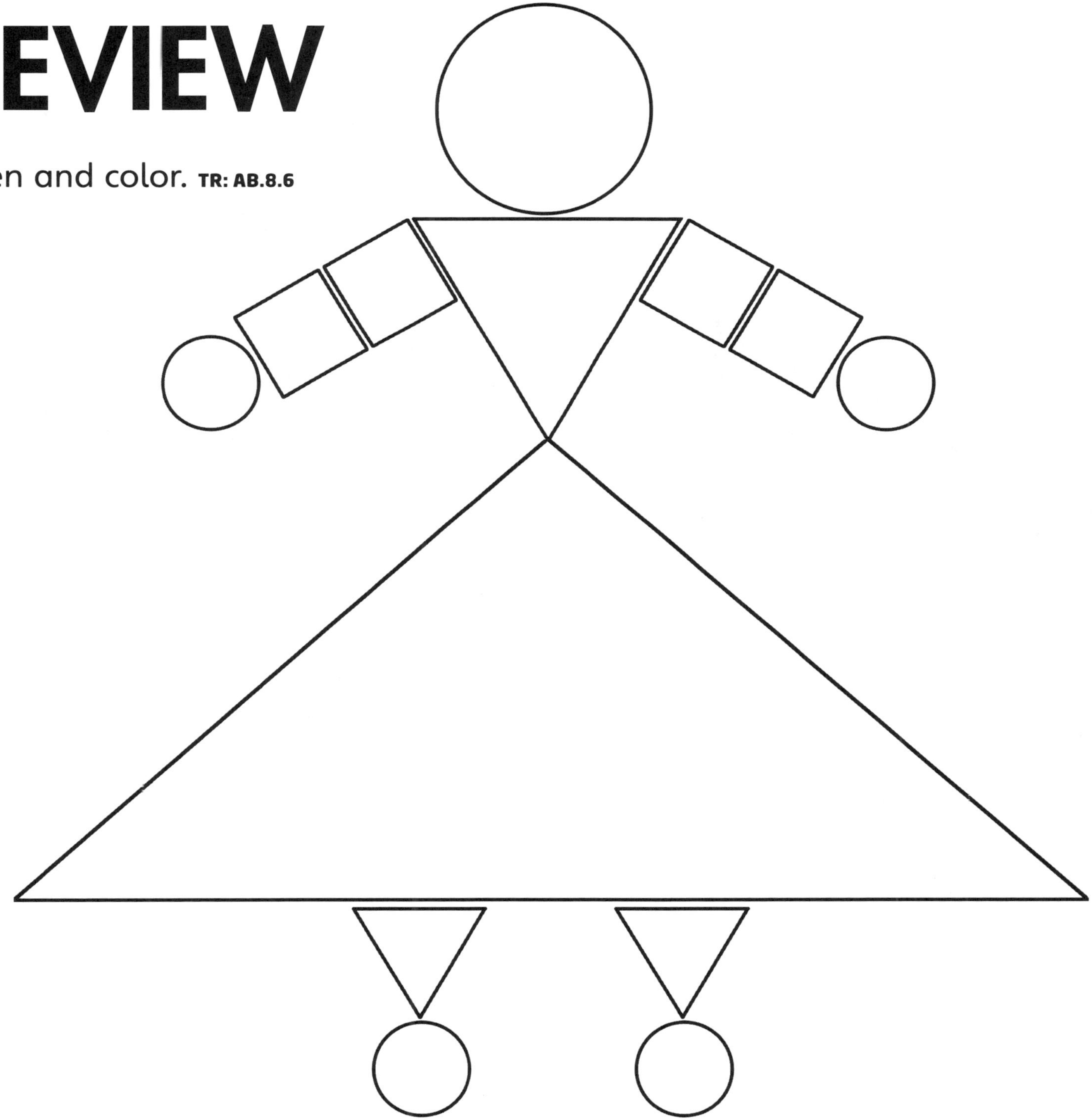

Find and trace. Say.

UNIT 1

REVIEW Count and say.

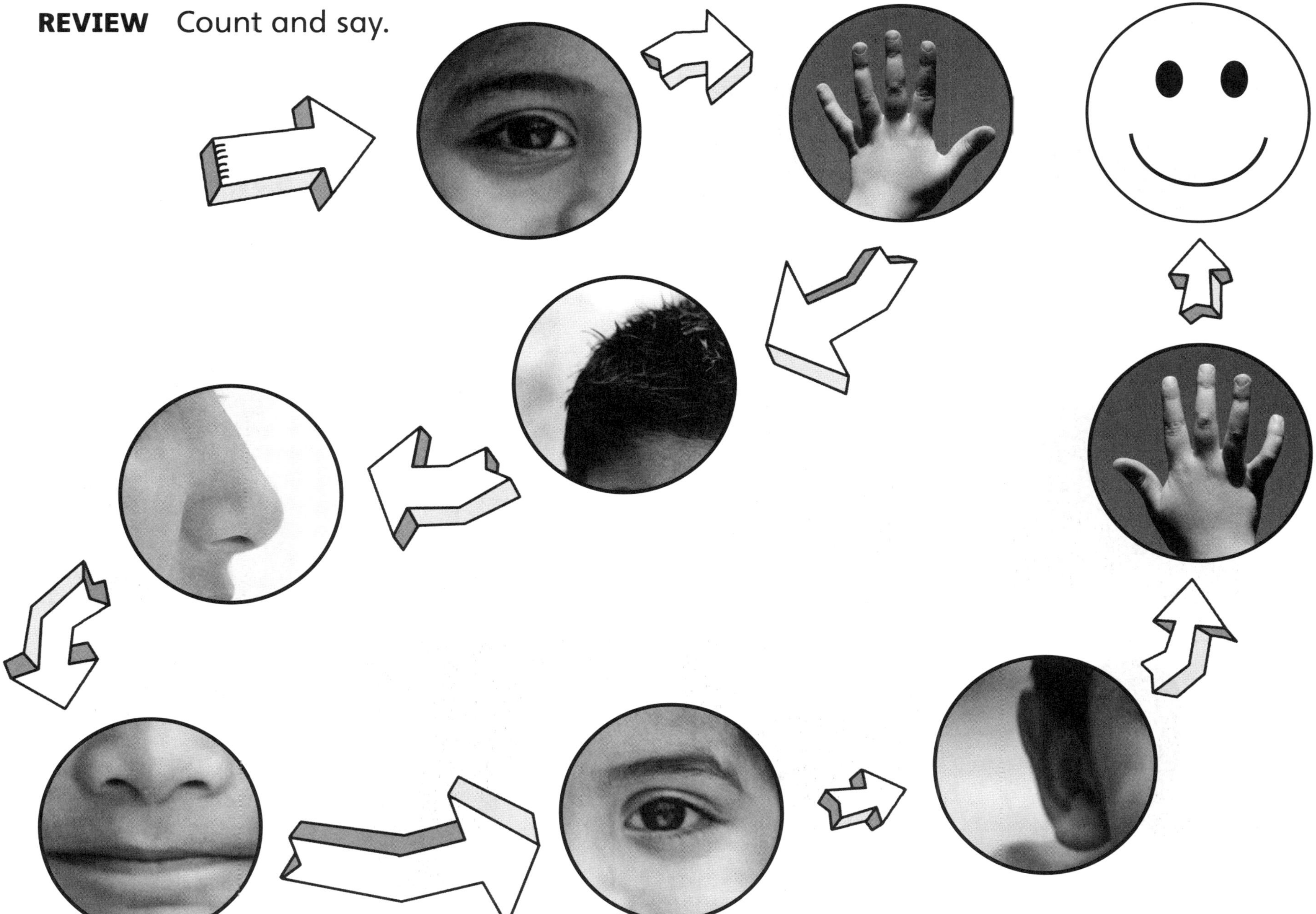

UNIT 2

REVIEW Listen and circle. Say. **TR: AB.2.4**

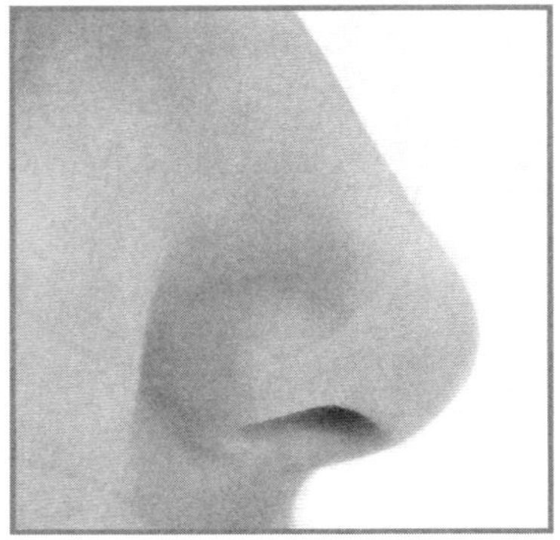
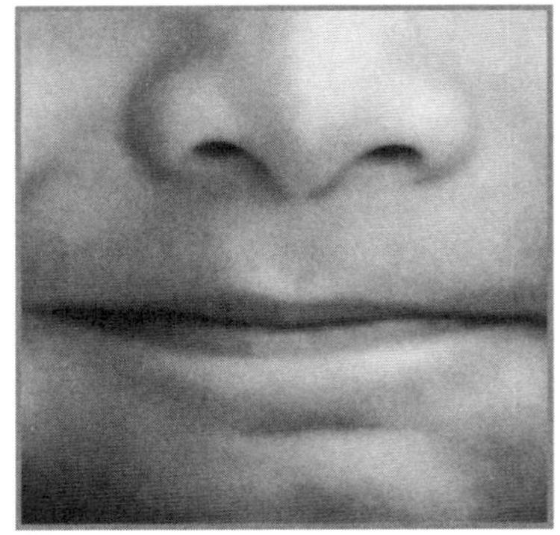
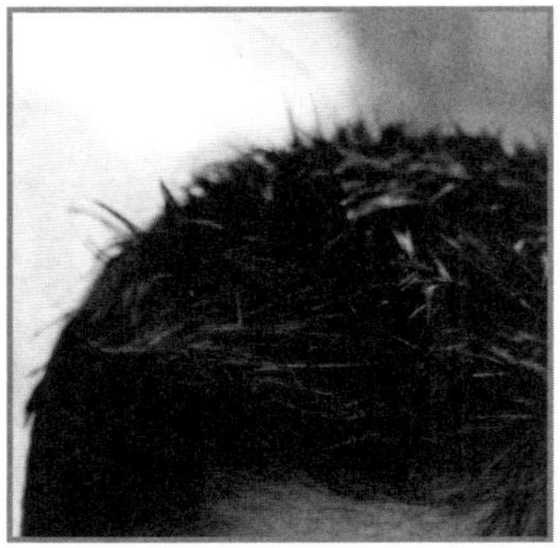

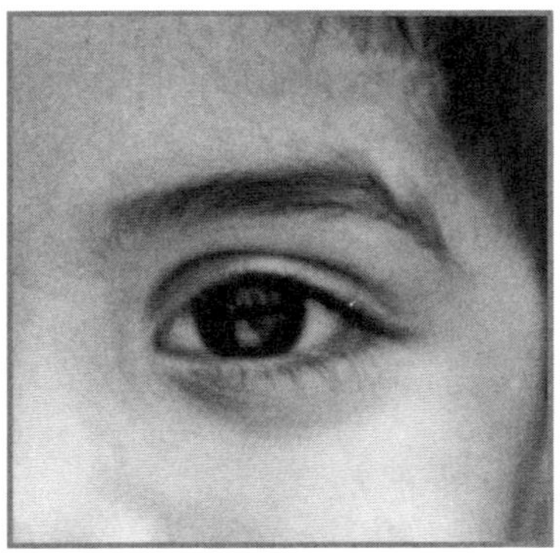
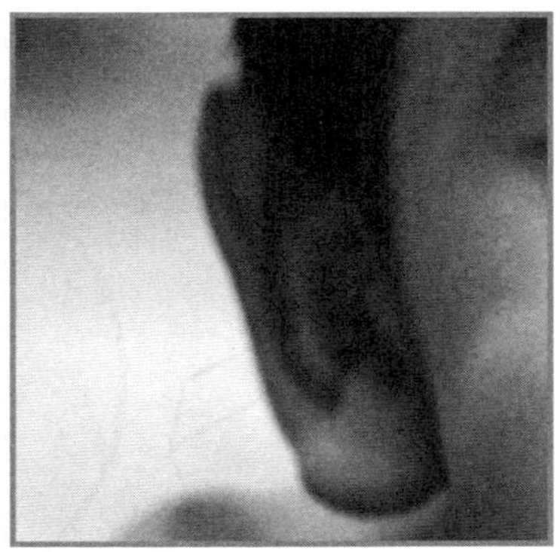

UNIT 3

REVIEW Find and count. Color.

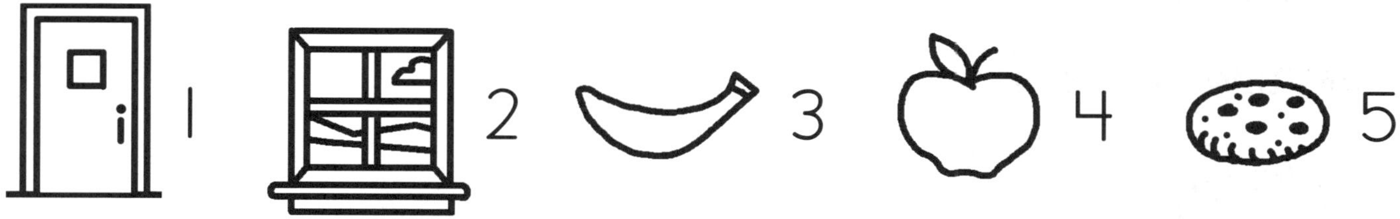

UNIT 4

REVIEW Look and say.

UNIT 5

REVIEW Look and draw a line. Say.

UNIT 6

REVIEW Count and say.

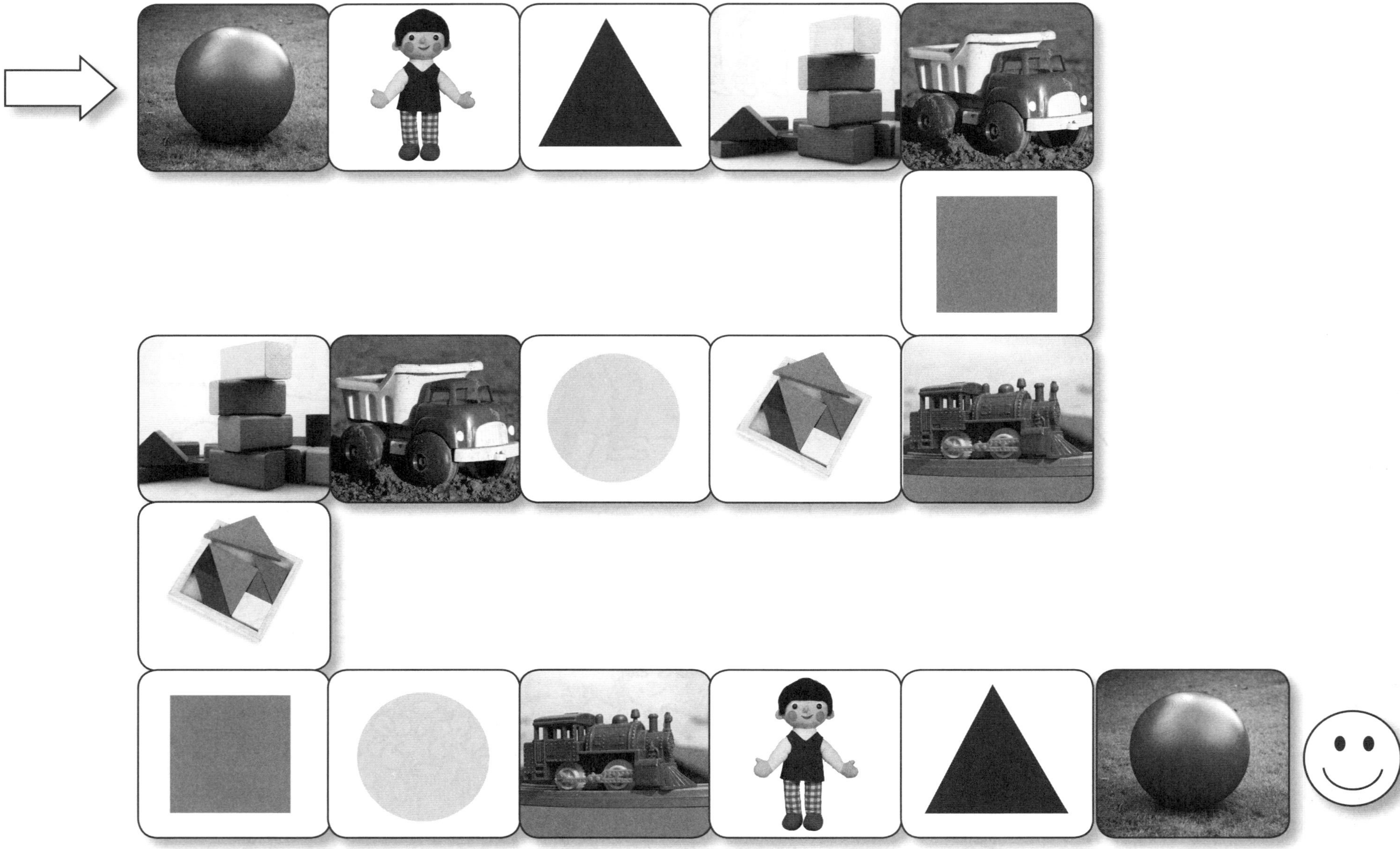

UNIT 7

REVIEW Draw a line and say.

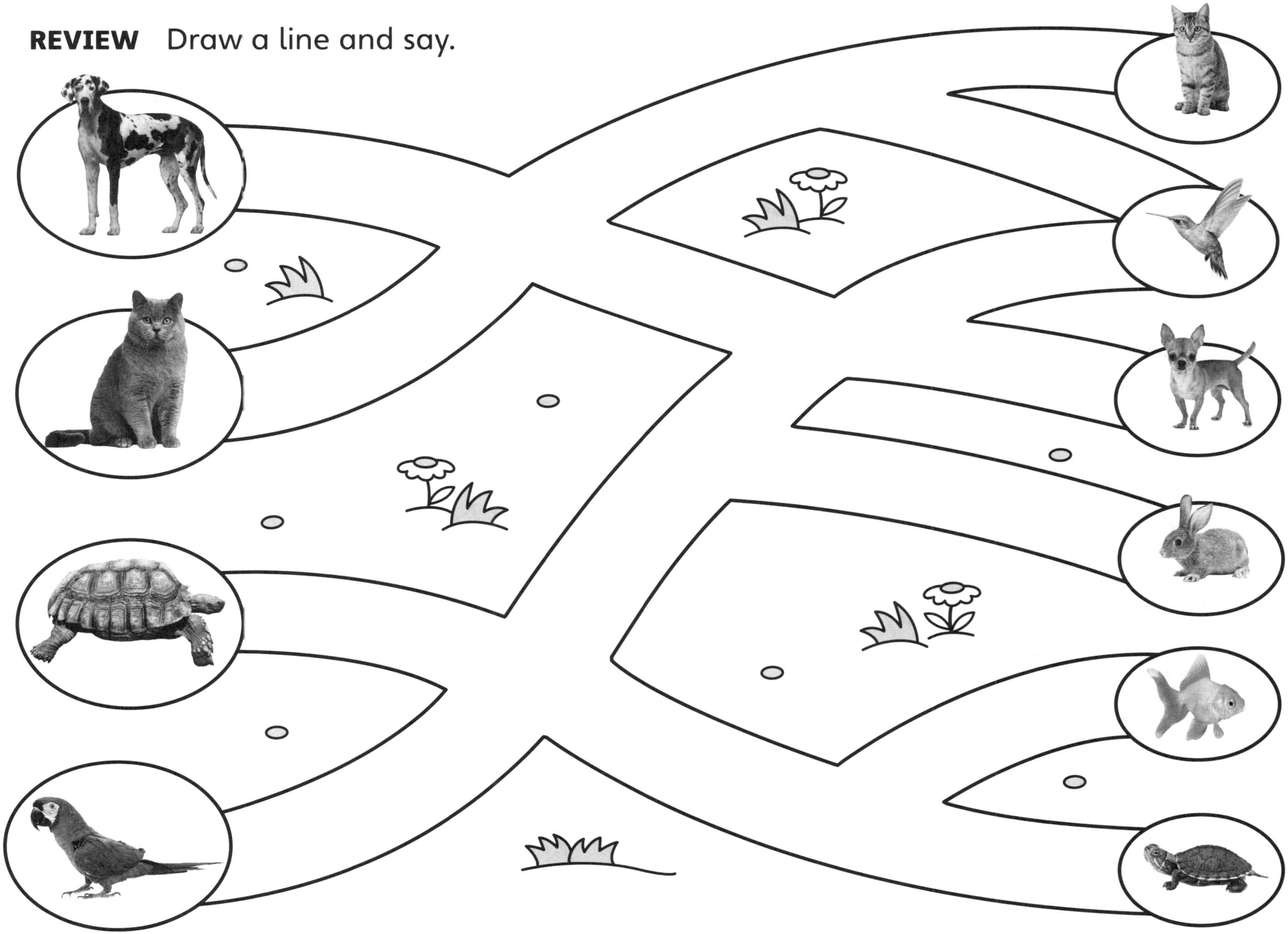

UNIT 8

REVIEW Listen and say. Listen and color. **TR: AB.8.4, AB.8.5**

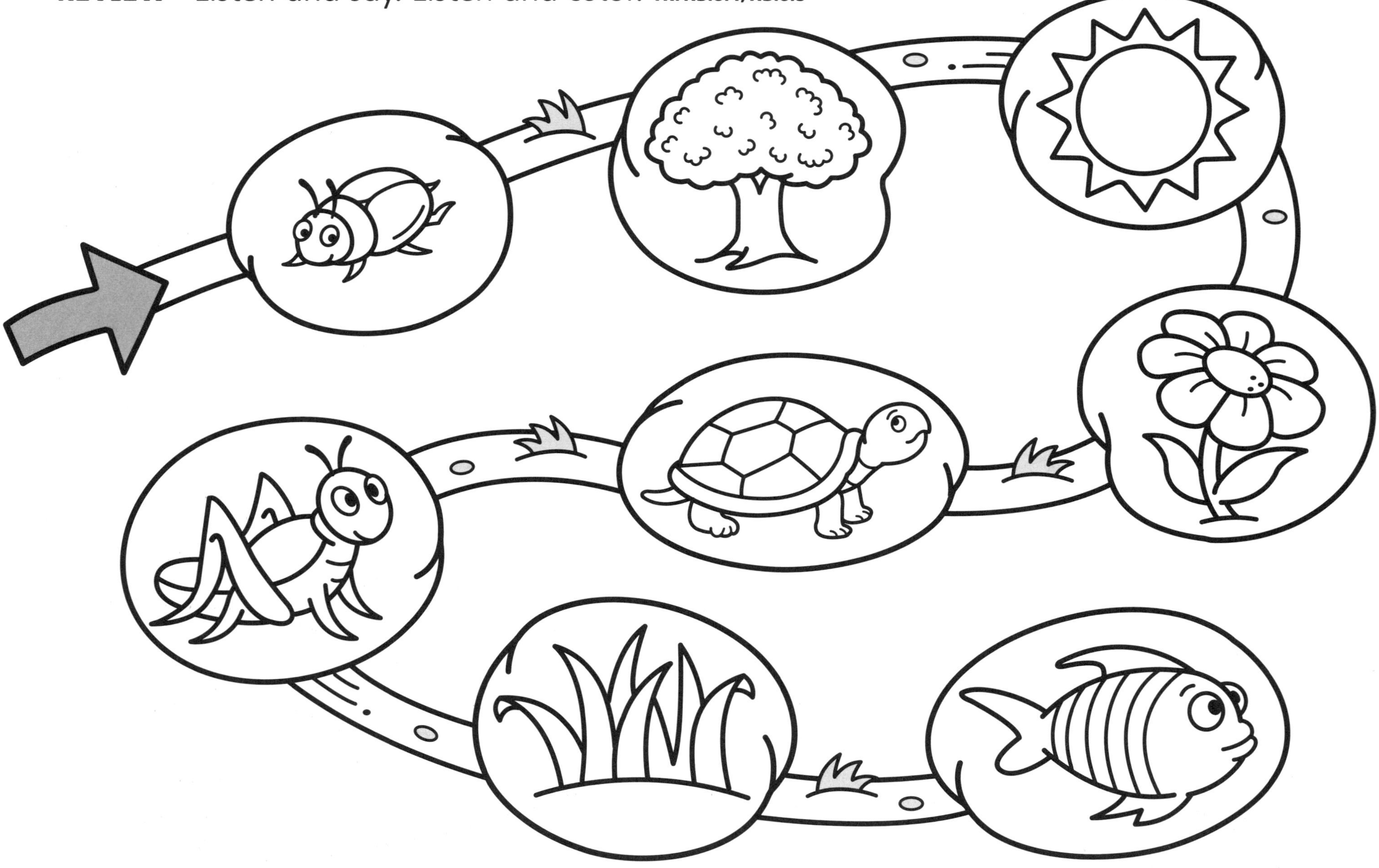